I should have been in bed by now

Tyvin Haque

Presentation by *BookLeaf Publishing*

Web: www.bookleafpub.com

E-mail: info@bookleafpub.com

ISBN: 9789357442275

First edition 2023

To the dreamer

Red

Red concrete laughter ringing
Bare feet on cold floor
Dancing in the rain
Twirling and swirling
Pitter patter on concrete
The taste of monsoon
Droplets hitting, faces smiling
Anklets ring
Speaking to the bells of rickshaw
Laughing and dancing
Twirling and swirling

Afterglow

Storm brewing
angry and resentful
lines that were blurred
Full of pain and tears

The storm answered in a
thundering rage
riddled with guilt and shame

A bone deep chill
smudges of colours
reds yellows and greens

Storm brewing
questions left unanswered
why...
a broken whisper

Grey clouds
like a doom of oppression
she stood alone
welcoming the darkness
a comforting blanket

the skies open in a
thundering answer
a kinship

tip toe, a step
gaining rhythm
she danced, breaking shackles

the rain washing away the tears
cleansed
for she finally felt free

as the fog lifted
she stood
alone
busking in the afterglow

Two white birds

They fly in sync
aware of the other
They dance to the rhythm
a song of golden string
Forever, they said
soul etched together

They fly in sync
twirling in a lovers embrace
two white birds
They dance to the song
Promise of the golden string

Look up to the sky
coloured in blues and gold
Two white birds
They dance to the song
A golden string

Two white birds
twirling in a lovers embrace
they found the shimmering
rainbow

I see you

To the child who
Could never be
A dreamer
Full of hope and light
She stood
Alone, wings clipped
I see you

I will hold you
As you heal
The little girl with
The brightest smile
The hope that shines through your eyes
I see you

Grown
She is brave
She is light
Her wings healed
I see you, fly

Sky

Look up to the sky
So blue and bright
On a winters day
Cold breeze
It brings hope
For spring is just
Out if touch

snowfall

7

Snowfalls as sun shines,
bright blue sky
so sharp, it stings
my skin
breathe in the air
thick and harsh

Memory

8

So fleeting
Yet its power
Holds us hostage
Like a movie
It dances just at the edge
Eyes distant

Listen, sounds of whisper
Eyes closed, ears straining
Can you feel
The love
The sorrow
The joy

Do you remember, that time
A place or a name,
So fleeting
Yet the mind keeps a score

Slow down

9

Slow down, take a breath
A moment of stillness
Eyes closed, listen
Whispers that echos
through the silence

What do you hear?

Sun

Close your eyes
Feel the heat of the sun
On a cold winter morning

What do you see?

Is it the burning red
Colours change
Red orange and yellow
Back to red

Did you find the darkend spots
Like droplets
Do you see the shadows
How well they dance
Can you hear its song

Do you see the
Colors
Blues and purple
They fight to be seen

Do you feel seen?

Dance

Breathe in, Breathe out
And just dance
Let the body move
Close your eyes, and
Dance to the song
That sings to your soul
Just dance

Dance, till the heart is
Filled

Enough

You try to cut me with your words
But they can't touch me
You bring me down, yet
I still rise
You burn me, yet
I rise above the ashes
When will it be enough for you
Will I ever be enough for you?

I know now I am enough
I have always been enough

Breathe

13

Breathe in, breathe out
Close your eyes
Wrap your arms, around
Your body
Sway to rhythm, the
One that sings to your soul
Breathe in, breathe out

A new beginning

Let the tears wash away
The pain that you feel
Feel the sadness
For what is lost
But remember the moments
That brings you joy

Remember the feeling of
Arms wrapped around you
Safe in its cocoon
Let the tears wash away your pain

As this moment is start of
a new beginning

Rainbow

15

Rainbow in the sky
Blink your eyes,
It disappeared

Twinkling stars

16

Look up to the
Twinkling stars
They shine and blink,
whisper of hello
A little shy
But look long enough
They make themselves known

In love

17

Red painted lips
Body marked in
Tiger stripes
Displayed to be watched.

Take a look, what do you see
Are you falling
In love

Never forget

The hurt
The pain
The injustice
How long will it take
When will it be enough
When will our voices be heard
The change that will occur

The hurt
The pain
The injustice
Bodies painted red
Forever lost
When will it be enough

Voices cracking
Tears flooding the streets
We raise our hands, for the
Lives taken too soon

Screaming, hearts breaking
Do you hear our cries?
Do you feel our pain?
Do you feel our rage
To the injustice?

Lives forever lost
Never forgotten

Winter night

A cold winter night
Wind blowing, sky pink and blue
Half moon is shining

in darkness we dance

It's the sharpness of the swords
In darkness, in grey mist
Bodies rush
Moving with each other
Air so thick

Feel the wind in the dancing bodies
In darkness bodies gliding
The battle continues
Feel the sword cutting into thick air

We move together
Forget the world around us
Mixed in mist and sweat
The light sips in
Our heart

The city

orange clouds, indigo blue skies
moon shining, glittering stars
birds finding there way home
Blinking lights, of a city
that never sleeps
As I close my eyes
feeling the wind caressing my skin
the city finally
fades to sleep

Colours

Colours
they surround me, in
blue and pink,
red and green
bursts of sunshine yellow and
citrusy orange.

Colours
they surround me.
In the morning glow
it shines glittering pink
look long enough
and they welcome you
to their musing

Milton Keynes UK
Ingram Content Group UK Ltd.
UKHW020906061224
452240UK00014B/901